OHIO'S RAILWAY AGE  IN POSTCARDS

OHIO HISTORY AND CULTURE

OHIO'S RAILWAY AGE IN POSTCARDS

H. ROGER GRANT

THE UNIVERSITY OF AKRON PRESS
AKRON, OHIO

Copyright © 1996 by H. Roger Grant
All rights reserved

All inquiries and permissions requests should be addressed to the Publisher,
The University of Akron Press, Akron, OH 44325-1703.

Manufactured in the United States of America
FIRST EDITION 1996
01 00 99 98 97 96   5 4 3 2 1

LIBRARY OF CONGRESS CATALOGING IN PUBLICATION DATA
Grant, H. Roger, 1943–
Ohio's railway age in postcards / H. Roger Grant.
p.   cm.—(Ohio history and culture)
Includes bibliographical references (p.   –   ) and index.
ISBN 1-884836-19-4 (cloth : alk. paper)
1. Railroads—Ohio—History—Pictorial works.
2. Postcards—Ohio—History.   I. Title.   II. Series.
TF24.O3G73   1996
385'.09771—dc20
96-10771
CIP

The paper used in this publication meets the minimum requirements of
American National Standard for Information Sciences—
Permanence of Paper for Printed Library Materials, ANSI z39.48—1984.∞

For Claibourne E. Griffin
and the late
Robert W. Chilcote

CONTENTS

PREFACE ix

OHIO'S RAILWAY HERITAGE: STEAM RAILROADS 3
OHIO'S RAILWAY HERITAGE: INTERURBANS 15
THE OHIO RAILROAD POSTCARD 25

THE ALBUM

STEAM 31

ELECTRIC 167

NOTES 195
INDEX 199

PREFACE

Encouraged by the positive response to my book, *Railroad Postcards in the Age of Steam* (1994), I decided to continue my work on railroad picture postcards. It struck me that cards associated with my adopted state of Ohio offered a splendid opportunity to focus on one of the nation's banner railroad centers. The Buckeye State possessed substantial steam railroad mileage and was the heartland of electric interurbans. Ohio also had a diversity of carriers, both steam and electric. And all of this railroad activity peaked when picture postcards were in vogue.

I knew that a book on Ohio railroad postcards was not only significant but possible. As the result of my longtime collecting of public timetables and other related railroad ephemera, I became acquainted with a Bedford, Ohio, postcard enthusiast who specialized in Ohio railroad cards. The late Robert "Bob" Chilcote was an affable retired high school mathematics teacher who assembled a diverse group of cards, especially "real-photo" ones, and, before his death in December 1995, he willingly allowed me to use his holdings. In order to complete coverage of the Ohio railroad scene during its golden years, I contacted another avid collector, Ralph H. Delap, a friend from the Akron Railroad Club who lives in Minerva, Ohio, for additional cards, particularly those showing the human side of railroading. And a few illustrations have come from my modest holdings.

    The preparation of this book has been a pleasant experience. I was delighted with the assistance I received from Bob Chilcote and Ralph Delap. Also, it was gratifying to work with The University of Akron Press staff, Julia Gammon, Elton Glaser, and Marybeth Mersky. This recently established press has begun operations on a positive note, and I am pleased to be part of this formative period.

H. Roger Grant

The University of Akron

OHIO'S RAILWAY AGE  IN POSTCARDS

OHIO'S RAILROAD HERITAGE
STEAM RAILROADS

Ohioans have long been blessed with excellent transportation. Admittedly, pioneers endured poor-quality roads or "traces," but they benefitted from their proximity to the Ohio River and other navigable streams and to Lake Erie and the other Great Lakes. When the technology became available, residents spearheaded canal, steam railroad, and electric interurban development.

By the 1820s, Ohioans knew that existing roadways and waterways were inadequate for development of modern economic activity. Soon residents caught canal-building fever. Inspired by New York's immensely successful Erie Canal, the harbinger of a national transportation mania, Ohioans committed considerable public resources to "ditch digging." The two principal artificial waterways, the Ohio and Erie Canal and the Miami and Erie Canal, accelerated the state's growth during the pre–Civil War years.[1]

But it was steam railroads rather than canals that revolutionized transport in Ohio. The appearance of the iron horse hastened industrial takeoff; flanged wheels greatly stimulated commercial agriculture and diversified manufacturing and ended the remaining commercial isolation within the region. "Railroads will make the state into a truly productive Eden," opined a Cleveland businessman in the 1850s. "There is no better way to move goods and people. . . . The locomotive is a heaven-sent invention."[2]

Ohioans took considerable pride in claiming some of the earliest railroad projects of the Republic. The stillborn Ohio Canal and Steubenville Rail-way [sic] Company, authorized by the General Assembly in 1830, sought to open a "single or double rail-way or road" from Steubenville, on the Ohio River, westward to the Ohio & Erie Canal. While other "paper" projects surfaced during the early 1830s, Ohioans did not hear the sound of a locomotive whistle until 1835. In that year, the Erie & Kalamazoo Rail Road was built between Adrian, Michigan, and Toledo, and the Mad River & Lake Erie Rail Road opened between Monroeville and Sandusky. Yet the total mileage in the state stood at only thirty miles in 1840.[3]

Pioneer Ohio railroads resembled their counterparts in the East, especially New England. They often connected only a few communities, likely linking them to a waterway: lake, river, or canal. A broken and scattered pattern of rail lines resulted. But these circumstances rapidly changed in the Buckeye State.[4]

Although some Ohioans before the Civil War argued that the state possessed adequate transportation arteries (the Ohio River, the Great Lakes, two north-south canals, and the east-west National Road completed in the 1830s), the more dependable, speedier, and efficient railroad found ardent supporters. Several advantages were clear. For one thing, a railroad could operate year-round; the Miami Canal, for instance, was frozen one winter for forty-nine consecutive days. Railroads, moreover, were much faster. Canal traffic flowed at speeds of from two to four miles an hour, while railroads hauled freight and passengers at ten to thirty miles an hour. Railroads also provided more reliable and frequent service. The editor of the *Hocking Sentinel* in Logan nicely expressed anti-canal sentiment in 1852: "Canals are tedious and uncertain when in operation, and useless from November till May. They are moreover managed by politicians and necessarily mismanaged."[5]

The speed of construction pleased champions of "steamcar civilization." In 1850, the 575-mile rail net placed Ohio fifth among the states, and trackage increased fivefold during the decade. On the eve of the Civil War, Ohio's 2,946 miles ranked the state first in the country. Consequently, canal barges and steamboats fell victim to the railroad juggernaut.[6]

The Ohio railroad system continued to expand in the decades that followed the Civil War. Not only did the East's four great trunk roads, which included the Baltimore & Ohio, Erie, New York Central, and Pennsylvania, bridge the state, but these giants also acquired or constructed hundreds of miles of additional secondary and branch lines. "System building" highlighted railroading in Gilded Age Ohio.[7]

The Erie Railroad is a good example. While the core of this carrier served New York, the company assembled a several-thousand-mile, multistate system after the Civil War. The Erie leased the largely trans-Ohio Atlantic & Great Western Railway in the 1860s and added the Cleveland

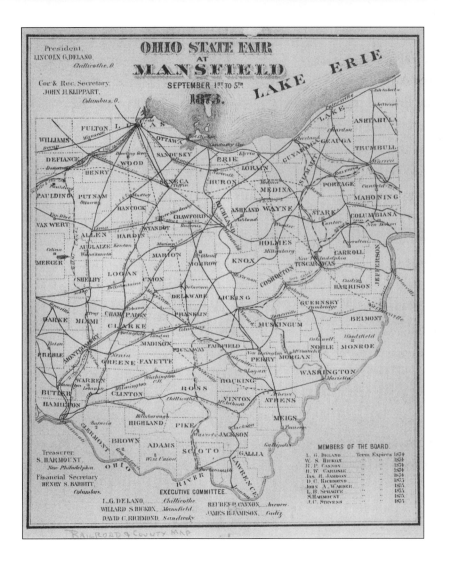

& Mahoning Valley Railroad a decade later. In the early 1880s, the Erie backed construction of the Chicago & Atlantic Railway, a property that gave it entry to Chicago from Marion, Ohio. By the 1890s, the Erie possessed a main line from Jersey City, New Jersey, to Chicago, serving the Ohio cities of Youngstown, Akron, Mansfield, Marion, and Lima. The company also controlled or leased strategic appendages to Cleveland, Dayton, and Cincinnati.[8]

Other carriers developed in Ohio during the post–Civil War "Railway Age." Typically, they were smaller ones: for example, the New York, Chicago & St. Louis ("Nickel Plate"); Toledo, St. Louis & Western ("Clover Leaf"); and the Wheeling & Lake Erie. Unlike most states during the late nineteenth and early twentieth centuries, Ohioans observed few independent short lines emerging. Those created commonly served a single industry or community. Two reasons account for the paucity of short lines: trunk roads met most of the public's basic transport needs; and, where problems existed, promoters favored electric interurbans.[9]

Ohio entered the twentieth century with a steam railroad mileage of 8,951; it peaked eight years later with 9,581 miles. While Illinois, Iowa, Pennsylvania, and Texas claimed more trackage, no state had a higher density of lines. Although the great boom had ended in Ohio with the Panic of May 1893, one important carrier opened in 1912, the eight-mile Akron, Canton & Youngstown Railroad (AC&Y). Promoted by the Goodyear Tire & Rubber Company, this industrial switching road failed to reach either Canton or Youngstown, yet expanded enormously in 1920 when it took over the moribund 162-mile Northern Ohio Railway (a New York Central property) that connected Fairlawn, west of Akron, with Delphos, northwest of Lima. A remarkable dimension of the AC&Y story was that this carrier, constructed late in the building history of area railroads, proved exceedingly profitable. Tough state and federal regulatory statutes, inspired by progressive era reformers, seemingly had little adverse effect on the AC&Y's balance sheets.[10]

While the Akron, Canton & Youngstown thrived, Ohio's steam railroads commonly felt the sting of motor competition after World War I. Ohioans frequently turned to their "tin lizzies" for their nearby journeys. Railroads were forced to reduce local passenger service and to close the smallest stations. Similarly, increased truck competition caused carriers to abandon lightly used appendages and to make other adjustments. Mileage shrank by nearly five hundred miles during the 1920s, and the subsequent Great Depression necessitated additional retrenchments.[11]

A major revival for the rails occurred during World War II. Ohioans rediscovered their hometown depots, not because their love of automobiles had waned but because stringent gasoline and tire rationing forced them to find alternative transportation. Freight customers, too, returned for largely the same reasons.[12]

With the coming of peace in 1945, the nation's railroads, prosperous for the first time in years, spent heavily to modernize their services. The most obvious example involved the replacement technology of the diesel-electric locomotive. The diesel revolutionized railroads, generating cheaper, faster, and more dependable operations. Not only did diesels become more numerous by the late 1940s in freight service, but early on they also powered the best passenger trains. After the war, Ohioans gained access to fleets of diesel-propelled "streamliners." Several railroads, most notably the Baltimore & Ohio, New York Central, and Pennsylvania, either replaced their old named passenger trains with modern lightweight equipment or inaugurated entirely new ones with state-of-the-art motive power and rolling stock.[13]

An illustration was the service offered by the Baltimore & Ohio. In promoting its *Capitol Limited*, a premier train that connected Chicago and Washington, D.C. with stops at Willard, Akron, and Youngstown, the company extolled its leadership in intercity travel: "First Air Conditioned! then Diesel Powered! then Streamlined!" In a 1949 advertising folder, the B&O described services on its flagship train: "A continuation of the same high standard of service, including Private Bedrooms, Drawing Rooms, Compartments and Section Sleepers; Colonial Dining Car, Lounge Car, Sunroom-Observation Car; Radio. Train Secretary, Valet, Maid-Manicure." The brochure added: "Air-Conditioned, of course—and Diesel-Power makes the ride so smooth, it's like gliding!"[14]

Yet by 1970 few passenger trains, whether crack or not, traveled Ohio rails. As elsewhere, these trains were casualties of increased automobile and airline usage. A much less opulent *Capitol Limited* made its final cross-state run in the spring of 1971. And its eventual namesake train (Chicago-Toledo-Cleveland-Washington) on Amtrak, the quasi-public National Railroad Passenger Corporation which made its debut on May 1, 1971, hardly equaled the luxury trains of the past.[15]

The recent Ohio railroad story contains fascinating historic twists. Just as state government once participated heavily in the sponsorship of canals, it belatedly re-entered the transportation field. Lawmakers created the Ohio Rail Transportation Authority (ORTA) in 1975 to oversee trackage that might be abandoned with dismemberment of the "Northeast Bankrupts." These railroads included two companies with extensive operations in Ohio, Penn Central (successor to the New York Central and Pennsylvania) and Erie Lackawanna (successor to the Erie). Congressional creation of the Consolidated Rail Corporation (Conrail) in 1976 led to a major restructuring of rail lines in Ohio, including the abandonment of much of the former Erie main stem. Portions of unwanted trackage were retained for shippers under ORTA supervision. By the mid-1990s, the state remained active in the railroad sector; it assisted public and private entities in acquiring threatened rail lines.[16]

During the past two decades, Ohio has experienced a proliferation of small railroad companies, reminiscent of the corporate pattern prior to system building. These new firms operate lines that major roads wished either to eliminate or to downgrade. The Coshocton-based Ohio Central illustrates this phenomenon. This carrier, launched in 1987, initially saved a one-time appendage of the Wheeling & Lake Erie in Stark, Tuscarawas, and Coshocton counties and a former Erie industrial switching operation in Mahoning County. Later the company acquired lines that had been part of the Baltimore & Ohio and Pennsylvania systems. By the mid-1990s, the Ohio Central claimed the status of a rail conglomerate, operating not only the Ohio Central Railroad, but also the Columbus & Ohio River Railroad, Ohio & Pennsylvania Railroad, Ohio Southern Railroad, Warren & Trumbull Railroad, and the Youngstown & Austintown Railroad.[17]

The present railroad map of Ohio reveals the presence of both the super carriers—Conrail, CSX, and Norfolk Southern, the latter two products of the megamergers of the 1980s—and thirty short lines. Not all of the World War II-era trackage has been retained. Mileage has dropped in recent decades to approximately 6,100. Nevertheless, Ohio remains one of the nation's greatest railroad bastions.[18]

The saga of Ohio railroads involves more than companies created and dissolved and mileage built and abandoned. More than any public transportation form, railroads have intimately involved people. For Ohioans in the nineteenth century, the steam railroad represented hope and progress. Whether rural or urban, individuals and communities that lacked access to adequate river, lake, or canal transport eagerly, even desperately, sought railway links. Whether a railroad came to a community or not often decided future prosperity and even survival. Not surprisingly, journalists filled their pages with tales of the rails. Even after the excitement of the arrival of the first train in Columbus had passed, the editor of the (Columbus) *Ohio Statesman* in 1850 remained excited about the Columbus & Xenia Rail Road:

> *Fine Excursions:* Among the pleasant afternoon excursions from our city, [nothing] holds out pleasanter inducements than leaving here in the cars at two o'clock and going as far as Xenia, spending a few hours and returning at 9 o'clock in the evening.

The run is over one of the best of Rail Roads and the finest of cars. Quite a company left this afternoon and will return this evening.[19]

The personal dimensions of railroading in Ohio are best seen in the past importance of the "dee-po." Whether the railroad station was in a bustling metropolis or a sleepy village, "train time" once meant much to the populace. Before internal combustion engines and modern communications, the depot provided contact with the outside world. Visitors and residents, newspapers and mail, express and freight passed through the facility. Furthermore, the station's chattering telegraph instruments offered the only means of quick communication. So important a place became a gathering site, especially in small communities, much like the barbershop, livery, or post office. During the railroad age, virtually everyone knew the location of the community's depot or depots, the name of the agent or agents, and the arrival and departure times of the important trains.[20]

The predominance of the steam railroad affected life in many ways. Ohioans named facilities to honor or recognize this extraordinary phenomenon. Scores of communities had a "Railroad Hotel," "Railroad Cafe," and "Railroad Avenue." There were also places that bore the name of some direct railroad association. Ohio had its share of "junctions" and "stations" attached to a particular town name. In the case of Chicago Junction, a division and repair point on the Baltimore & Ohio in Huron County, the community's name suggested its strategic railroad importance. Later, Chicago Junction changed its name to honor the longtime (1910–1941) and popular president of the company, Daniel Willard.[21]

And there were railroad jokes. The Erie Railroad, because of its several bankruptcies, became known as the "Weary Erie." There was the old wheeze: "I want to go to Chicago the worst way." "Take the Erie!" Employees and travelers commonly concocted humorous, even scathing, nicknames by recasting the initials of railroad companies. The Bellaire, Zanesville & Cincinnati, a narrow gauge railway, controlled by the Pennsylvania, with curves that were all but continuous, won an appropriate designation: Bent, Zigzag & Crooked. The Lake Erie & Western (LE&W), once part of the New York Central system, was dubbed the "Leave Early & Walk" route. The Pittsburgh, Fort Wayne & Chicago, a vital part of the future Pennsylvania system across the state, became "Pigs' Feet, Whisky & Cigars" (time has obscured the whimsy). And the Zanesville & Western, ultimately affiliated with the New York Central, emerged as the "Zealous & Willing."[22]

People, too, had fun with town names and used a railroad context for such humor. The copy on a comic postcard, published about 1905 as part of an "Ohio Whisperettes" series, went as follows:

> I wanted to go to Morrow, Ohio. I asked a man the quickest way to get to the depot. He said, RUN. When I reached the depot, there was a train on the side-track:—I asked the agent, "Does this train go to Morrow?" He said, "No, it goes to-day." I told him I wanted to go to Morrow. He said, "Come down tomorrow and go." I told him I wanted to go to Morrow to-day. Just as the train was pulling out, I said, "IS THIS MY TRAIN?" He said, "No, the R.R. Co. wants to use it." I went way back and sat down on a truck, telling the agent he was too fresh. He said, so was the paint on the truck.[23]

OHIO'S RAILROAD HERITAGE
INTERURBANS

Just as steam railroads had excited Americans, "interurban fever" spread rapidly after 1900. This was the era of the newly perfected electric traction railway. "Tracks! Tracks! It seemed to the visionaries of that day that the future lay at the end of parallel rails," recounted novelist E. L. Doctorow in his bestseller *Ragtime*. "There were long-distance interurban railroads, laying their steel stripes on the land, crisscrossing like the texture of an indefatigable civilization."[24]

As the result of improved technology and a healthy economy, intercity electric mileage burgeoned following the Spanish-American War. While less than a thousand miles existed in 1897, that total exceeded more than ten thousand miles a decade later; the country's interurban network peaked at slightly over fifteen thousand miles in 1915. Electric lines laced large sections of the nation, especially in New England and the Old Northwest. In fact, Ohio and Indiana became the heartland of "compressed air." With lines radiating out of all the large- and medium-size cities, the respective traction maps of these two states resembled plates of wet spaghetti. Yet electric roads also appeared in more remote sections of the country, connecting such isolated communities as Warren and Bisbee, Arizona, and Sheridan and Monarch, Wyoming.[25]

The popularity of electric traction is understandable. If a community or region lacked adequate steam rail service, an interurban could solve the problem. Traction routes allowed farmers, miners, and others convenient access to opportunities offered by urban centers, and in turn these communities could profitably tap a wider trading area. Electric lines typically maintained convenient schedules, often hourly, rather than one or two times daily as did steam roads. Moreover, interurbans, unlike steamcars, would stop virtually anywhere. Differing, too, from steam-powered trains, interurbans were clean, producing "no cinders, no dirt, no dust, no smoke." And they were potentially fast. If the roadbed and operating conditions allowed, an electric car could accelerate within seconds to sixty or more miles per hour. Interurban operators, particularly in the Old Northwest and the trans-Mississippi West, frequently entered the trolley-freight business and served customers who perhaps lacked a rail connection. The traveling and shipping public also welcomed less expensive rates for passenger, express, and freight service. This was especially appreciated after years of widespread discontent with steam railroad charges. This new mode of transportation, with all of its advantages, also attracted riders because the horse-drawn buggy and wagon had drastic limitations. Even with the coming of the automobile and truck, highway travel remained primitive. It would take years for the good-roads movement to lift the nation out of the mud and dust.[26]

Ohioans pioneered electric intercity traction. Although Richmond, Virginia, was the place where the feasibility of an electric railroad was demonstrated in 1887, the Buckeye State quickly entered the realm of electric-powered transport. Ohio has a legitimate claim of being the "first" in this field: in 1889, a seven-mile electric line began operations between Newark and Granville. While admittedly this central Ohio road resembled a rural trolley, the undeniable prototype of the modern, high-speed interurban opened between Akron and Cleveland six years later. The agency of this advance, the Akron, Bedford & Cleveland Railroad, "The Alphabet Route," with its extensive private right-of-way, was built largely to steam railroad standards.[27]

An interurban building boom followed. Between 1897 and 1915, Ohio's electric intercity network soared from less than a hundred miles to nearly three thousand. Only Indiana with a 1,825-mile network made a comparable commitment to electric traction. Conditions in Ohio were ideal. With the exception of the Ohio River counties, the topography of the state was often either flat or gently rolling, which greatly reduced construction and operating costs. Ohio also possessed a large population: the 1900 census reported 4,157,545 residents, making the state the fourth most populous in the nation. Many of these people lived in medium-sized and closely spaced cities. Ohio also had several robust urban centers, a well-settled countryside, and bustling coal mining camps that dotted the southeastern section. Not only did the state offer an attractive landscape and population mixture, but the overall level of prosperity was also high. While the depression of the mid-1890s caused some painful economic dislocations, the state rapidly regained its financial health.[28]

Residents of Ohio quickly sensed the arrival of the interurban era. For one thing, they were ex-

posed to the much-publicized "golden spike" ceremony held in Findlay on December 31, 1905. On that early winter day, scores of well-wishers—traction company executives, industry leaders, politicians, journalists and the curious—gathered in that west-central community of 17,613 to witness the "official" joining of the Toledo, Bowling Green & Southern Traction Company and the Western Ohio Railway. The former connected Findlay with Toledo and the latter Findlay with Lima. The meeting of the two "juice" roads held considerable significance: it heralded the closing of the gap between interurban lines of northeastern and southern Ohio. Indirectly, this gala affair marked the linkup of interurbans in four states. "Last spike in the link connecting Pennsylvania, Ohio, Michigan and Indiana electric railways" were the words inscribed on the ceremonial spike.[29]

So phenomenal was interurban expansion throughout the nation, including Ohio, that, as the first decade of the twentieth century ended, it was possible to take electric cars for much of the distance between New York City and Chicago. To demonstrate the maturity of the industry, an official of the Interborough Rapid Transit Company of New York City, J. S. Moulton, undertook such a trip in 1909. Moulton realized that the day of the isolated interurban had passed. Ohio, of course, became a central part of his traction odyssey.

> At 7 o'clock [a.m.] . . . I started over the road of the Conneaut & Erie Traction Company [from Erie, Pennsylvania] for Conneaut, a distance of 33 miles, arriving there at 8:55 a.m. A wait of 30 minutes gave me time to set back my watch one hour, as I was travelling then on western [Central Standard] time. Leaving Conneaut at 9:30 a.m. on the Pennsylvania & Ohio Railway, I travelled to

Ashtabula and there took a car of the Cleveland, Painesville & Eastern via Painesville, for Cleveland. The distance from Conneaut to Cleveland is 73 miles. Cleveland was reached at 12:50 p.m. and after lunch I left at 1:30 p.m. on a limited car of the Lake Shore Electric Railway for Toledo, a distance of 120 miles, via Sandusky, which was made in four hours and 20 minutes without change [of equipment]. After supper at Toledo, I went to the terminal of the Ohio Electric Railway and took the 8 p.m. car of that company for Fort Wayne, Ind., via Lima, Ohio. As I did not leave Toledo until so late I did not stay on the car until Fort Wayne was reached, but thought it better to stop at Lima, where I arrived at 10:55 p.m.

On the following morning . . . [I] took the 10:15 a.m. [Ohio Electric] car . . . , a distance of 60 miles to Fort Wayne, which was reached at 12:10 p.m. At Van Wert, Ohio, the Manhattan Limited of the Pennsylvania Railroad, which parallels the electric line at this point, came up, but we passed the steam train and kept ahead of it. At Fort Wayne I had dinner. . . .[30]

Aware of the need for closer ties, cooperation became a hallmark of Ohio interurbans. A majority of local electric roads banded together in 1904 to launch the Ohio Interurban Railway Association, and Indiana soon responded with a similar organization. Then, in 1906, representatives from the two groups formed the Central Electric Railway Association (CERA). Initially, the CERA represented thirty-eight major interurbans that operated in these two states. The association, while lacking legally binding powers, advocated frequent-traveler mileage discount books, created a tariff bureau, and provided maps, timetables, and publicity. Eventually, the CERA added additional Ohio and Indiana interurbans and also some from Kentucky and Michigan.[31]

While the Central Electric Railway Association represented successful interurban projects, the

Ohio Electric Railway

BETWEEN
FT. WAYNE AND LIMA

4 Limited Trains Each Way Daily

2 Hours Time 65 Miles

FARE REDUCED TO ONE DOLLAR

No Excess Fare on Limiteds   150 Pounds of Baggage Free

LAND YOU IN BUSINESS DISTRICT

Leave Ft. Wayne---East								Leave Lima---West					
	a. m.	a. m.	a. m.	p. m.	p. m.	p. m.	p. m.		a. m.	a. m.	a. m.	p. m.	p. m.	p. m.
Limiteds		8:20	10:20		2:20	4:20		Limiteds		8:15	10:15		2:15	4:15
Locals	7:05	9:05	11:05	1:05	3:05	5:05	8:05	Locals	7:05	9:05	11:05	1:05	3:05	5:05	8:05

For Full Information and Time Tables Ask Ticket Agents or Address

W. S. WHITNEY, G. P. & F. A., Columbus, Ohio   F. A. BURKHARDT, D. P. & F. A., Lima, Ohio

story of electric railways in the Buckeye State also involved unbuilt or "paper" roads. In the heyday of traction excitement, scores of proposed routes came to the public's attention. Some merely fell into the "good idea" category: no serious effort was made to obtain a charter, to make line surveys, or to seek commitments from investors. One ill-fated scheme, discussed in 1906 and 1907, championed an interurban between Fostoria, Upper Sandusky, and Marion. Some companies, like the Galion Southern (Galion to Fredericktown), completed their legal work, acquired rights-of-way, and even raised capital, but never turned a wheel. Established interurbans similarly proposed extensions that failed to materialize. The Akron-based Northern Ohio Traction & Light Company hoped to span the forty-six miles from its southern terminus at Uhrichsville to Wheeling, West Virginia, but it never did.[32]

By World War I, the interurban era had peaked in Ohio and elsewhere. Marginally profitable roads revealed their vulnerability to automobile competition. Following the war, not only had the production of motor vehicles escalated, but the overall condition of the state's roadways had also greatly improved. Typical of the early wave of casualties was the Columbus, Magnetic Springs & Northern Railway (CMS&N). This modest operation opened in 1904 between Delaware and Magnetic Springs, a distance of eleven miles. Two years later the company completed a seven-mile extension northwestward to Richwood, but it never expanded further. Always financially weak, the CMS&N, like so many interurbans, valiantly tried to save itself by attracting pleasure seekers, but the spas at Magnetic Springs fizzled. Automobiles and all-weather roads in Delaware and Union counties killed the "Magnetic Springs Route"; the last car clanked over the weedy line on New Year's Day 1919.[33]

Few Ohio interurbans succeeded in developing a profitable freight business. Some bravely tried during the 1920s, but anticipated profits were never realized. Even the admonition of the Toledo, Fostoria & Findlay Railway in the late 1920s to "SHIP YOUR FREIGHT BY THE INTERURBANS AND SAVE THE HIGHWAYS" had no apparent impact. It is understandable that Ohio's last interurban, the Youngstown & Southern, developed a substantial business hauling coal to greater Youngstown steel mills. The company dieselized in the late 1940s and remained active until the early 1990s.[34]

Although the long-term story of Ohio's interurban era was one of common financial failure, the state benefitted from this form of intercity transport. The impact on economic development was considerable; the interurban served as the transitional link between the steam road and the motorized vehicle for passenger and express traffic. But the state's electric roads at times proved more than a convenient, comfortable, and economic means of transport. A number of companies profitably entered the commercial power business. Since interurbans often constructed their own generating plants, substations, and transmission lines, these firms sold their excess electrical capacity. The cover of the Northwestern Ohio Railway & Power Company timetable for spring 1916 illustrated this initiative: "Electric Current. We are supplying current in any quantity. Make application to Superintendent or General Manager for rates, etc." In some cases, commercial electric sales "saved" the interurban investor.[35]

Physically, little remains of Ohio's once vigorous interurban network. Only tiny segments of the Youngstown & Southern and a few other carriers survive. Some pieces of rights-of-way have become biking, hiking, or nature trails, but most that have survived are choked with brush and memories. A knowledgeable observer can occasionally spot a former interurban depot, substation, bridge abutment, or even a rail protruding from a city street. It is ironic that modern commuters, who frequently encounter traffic gridlock, follow routes once served by the "wave of the future," the electric interurban railway.[36]

THE OHIO RAILROAD POSTCARD

A picture postcard craze burst upon Ohio and the nation early in the twentieth century. This "postal carditis," set off by "pioneer" cards celebrating the World's Columbian Exposition in Chicago in 1893, benefitted greatly from a decision of the Post Office Department in 1898. Privately printed postcards could henceforth be mailed at the same rate as government issues, at one cent each. Public pressure for further changes in the use of picture postcards came in 1907. Senders could thereafter write messages on the *reverse* side of the card; previously, only the address could appear there. "Divided" or "split" cards stimulated a card mania that climaxed shortly before World War I.[37]

It is not surprising that railroad images became popular. After all, this was the heyday of the passenger train. The railroad was the means by which most people traveled, the practical way to cover long distances. Significantly, the depot served as a focal point of community life, and these structures were abundant in the Buckeye State. The Ohio Commissioner of Railroads and Telegraphs reported in 1888 that the state had 2,199 of these specialized structures, noting that seven were stone, eighty-five brick, and the remainder of wooden construction. The number of depots, in fact, reached its zenith at precisely the time of intense interest in picture postcards. Predictably, cardmakers pictured depots more than anything else associated with steam railways. These structures wonderfully symbolized the community, as much or more so than churches, public buildings, or monuments. But producers also printed numerous views of trains and scenes along the railroad corridor.[38]

The rage for picture postcards also coincided with the interurban era. Cardmakers especially liked the electric car. Although traction roads owned depots, they were seldom attractive. Many stations were located in commercial store fronts and hotel lobbies, and some were nothing more than shelters at trackside.

Producers of picture postcards sometimes invented spurious interurban images. At a time when boosters demanded "compressed air" for their hometowns, some felt hurt, even discouraged, by the absence of electric traction. If Coshocton, the largest community in Ohio without an interurban, could not have the "real McCoy," a card with an interurban car, rails, poles, and overhead wire might lessen the distress. At least one commercial photographer, who specialized in making bogus cards of midwestern towns, altered a Coshocton street scene—and perhaps prospered in the process.[39]

When selecting an appropriate railroad-related picture postcard, customers enjoyed a variety of real or imagined scenes, but the quality itself varied. In the largest communities, retailers, who might sell their wares (perhaps thousands of cards weekly) from a stationery shop, specialized card store, or souvenir stand, could offer delicately colored views, often the handiwork of skilled German artisans. In the smallest places, buyers usually found only the cheaper black-and-white cards in the drugstore or general store. The merchant had likely arranged with a printer to convert local photographs into a limited quantity of "real-photo" cards. The restricted market could not justify the expense of color cards or even ones printed in a somewhat more attractive fashion.[40]

If the desired card were unavailable, individuals could design their own. Exploiting the growing popularity of picture postcards, the Eastman Kodak Company introduced a special postcard camera in 1903. The photographer snapped the shutter and, if desired, could use a stylus to write a short caption on the exposed postcard-size film ($3\frac{1}{4}$ by $5\frac{1}{2}$ inches). The final process, which usually required commercial assistance, involved making a contact print on the appropriate postcard stock. A year earlier, Kodak put on the market a heavy photographic paper on which images could be easily, effectively, and cheaply printed from negatives.[41]

Ohioans clearly liked picture postcards, whether commercial or not, for a variety of reasons. Some enjoyed collecting and mounting them in albums, which they could show to family and friends or keep for their own pleasure. A postcard conveyed what a particular site, event, or person looked like. Illustrations in newspapers and magazines were few, and a card could satisfy a personal desire or curiosity. If the "flyer" derailed nearby, individuals might buy a card or set of cards from an enterprising local photographer, or they might produce their own.[42]

Picture postcards pleased senders; the cards could be quickly written and mailed. While letter writing had its faithful adherents, many appreciated the limited space, even with the 1907 reform, that a card provided. "This sure beats writing a letter," noted an Akronite in 1909. "Im [sic] glad that You and Mother [are] coming for church & dinner." Some commentators believed that the card craze endangered the art of letter writing, including love letters.[43]

Picture postcards were highly practical. For about a nickel (the cost of the card and postage), a card could be sent, often with astonishing results. In an age before extensive long-distance telephone service and when telegrams were sent only in emergencies, the public discovered that the card functioned very well for quick communication. It was common for a card, mailed at the post office or in the slot of a Railway Post Office car standing in the station, to arrive at its local destination or in nearby communities either later the same day or the next. The rapidity with which cards were delivered can be explained both by fast mail trains which provided sorting en route and the practice of "putting up" mail in the post office soon after the sacks reached the community. Residents of cities customarily received twice-daily home delivery (Monday through Friday), and the commercial sections of major metropolises, Cleveland and Cincinnati, for example, had three-times-daily service during the workweek.[44]

The picture postcard craze had mostly run its course by 1920. Following the war, people preferred to take "snaps" and not bother with the postcard-making process, even though postcard film remained available for decades. Still, commercial cards continued to be produced. But the later images lacked the quality of earlier ones. "Linens" and then "chromes" of subsequent decades were hardly aesthetic gems. The amateur but spontaneous character of the real-photo cards was gone. Collecting diminished until nostalgia in recent years spurred a keen interest in historic cards.[45]

There were other changes, too, especially for the railroad-related picture postcard. Railroad subjects, whether in Ohio or elsewhere, faded in popularity. After all, the railway age and the interurban era had largely passed; both were mostly gone by 1930. If Ohioans bought transportation cards, they turned to those associated with airplanes, automobiles, and buses. Of course, cards of public buildings and tourist sites remained in demand, whether the picture was of the state capitol in Columbus or Cedar Point, the amusement park in Sandusky, and the "Having fun, wish you were here" messages continued. Still, whether as cheap souvenirs of a vacation trip or as charming evocations of an era long past, the picture postcard maintains its fascination for many people.

OHIO'S RAILWAY AGE  IN POSTCARDS

STEAM

UNION STATION & HIGH ST., COLUMBUS, OHIO.
Published by The Nitschke Paper Co., Columbus, O. Made in Germany.

DEPOTS

1. Patrons of railroads which used Union Station in Columbus enjoyed access to an ornate beaux arts–inspired structure. While this facility lacked the status of a true "union" or consolidated station, trains of the Baltimore & Ohio, Hocking Valley, Norfolk & Western, and Pennsylvania railroads served this facility. (Chilcote)

2. Passenger trains of the Toledo & Ohio Central, a New York Central affiliate, arrived and departed from this architecturally eclectic depot, located a mile and a quarter from Columbus Union Station. (Chilcote)

3. The five steam roads that served the southwestern Ohio metropolis of Dayton used an impressive Romanesque station, opened early in the 20th century. (Chilcote)

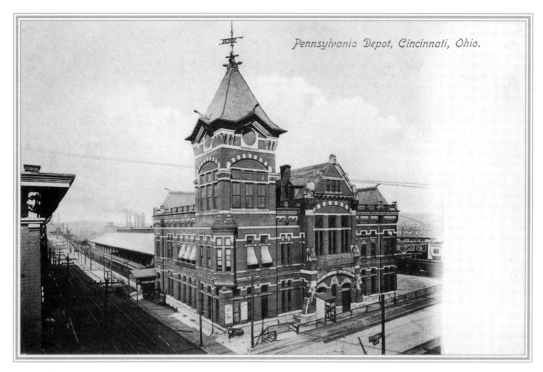

4. The "Pennsylvania Depot" in Cincinnati hosted more than trains of the mighty Pennsylvania system. The Louisville & Nashville and Norfolk & Western occupied the facility before completion of Union Station in the early 1930s. (Chilcote)

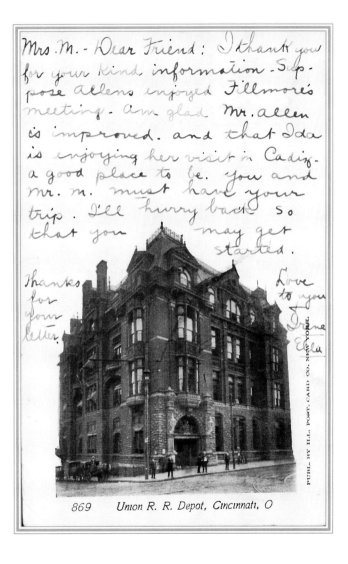

5. The immediate predecessor to Cincinnati's art deco Union Station was the ornate Central Union Depot, located at West 3rd and Central Avenue, which opened on April 9, 1883. (Chilcote)

6. One of America's great railway stations was Cleveland's Union Terminal, built in the late 1920s and designed by the architectural firm of Graham, Anderson, Probst and White. The Cleveland terminal sported a superimposed office building, an unusual feature, which made this 708-foot structure the tallest building outside New York City until 1967. A postcard view reveals the ticketing area about the time the facility opened. (Delap)

7. Residents of smaller Ohio communities might brag about their "union" depot. Those who lived in Crestline could meet trains of the Cleveland, Cincinnati, Chicago & St. Louis or "Big Four" (New York Central) and Pennsylvania at this rambling three-story L-shape brick structure. (Chilcote)

8. Although three depots once served Bellaire, the one constructed by the Pennsylvania was a sizable affair. The second story likely housed offices for operating personnel. (Chilcote)

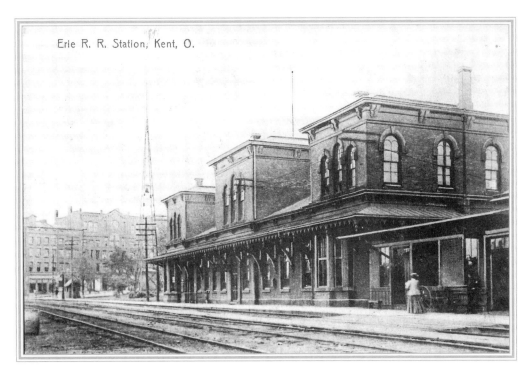

9. Residents of Kent surely admired the architecture of their Erie depot, built by predecessor Atlantic & Great Western. Kent was a division point on the Erie's New York-Chicago main line and the company needed the upper level office space. (Chilcote)

10. A depot of a vintage similar to the one at Kent stood along the Baltimore & Ohio line in Newark. Again, second-story space accommodated operating personnel. (Chilcote)

11. The Baltimore & Ohio made Willard (neé Chicago Junction) in Huron County the hub of its mid-Ohio railway operations. This brick depot remained in service until the 1960s. (Chilcote)

12. The "Panhandle Division" of the Pennsylvania Railroad possessed a two-story depot in the Ohio River city of Steubenville. The low extension on the side elevation likely sheltered freight and express operations. The single-story depot in the background probably belonged to the Wheeling & Lake Erie Railroad. (Chilcote)

13. A modern depot served patrons of the Norfolk & Western in Portsmouth. The city's two other railroads, Baltimore & Ohio and Chesapeake & Ohio, each owned separate facilities. The reverse side of this 1930-era card contains this inscription: "The N.& W. R.R. Terminals are located in Portsmouth. 5,000 contented workmen are employed." (Chilcote)

14. Only a handful of Ohio communities possessed a depot with an apartment for the agent and his family. Since the state never faced an acute housing shortage during the Railway Age, living-in-the-depot arrangements were deemed unnecessary. The Pennsylvania, however, erected a two-story depot to accommodate its agent in the Wayne County village of Shreve. (Chilcote)

15. The Baltimore & Ohio erected several depots in Ohio with living quarters for agents. The facility at Greenwich in Huron County offered these accommodations. (Chilcote)

16. It is possible that the Baltimore & Ohio constructed a depot with upstairs living space in the Perry County mining community of Shawnee. (Chilcote)

17. The agent peers out of this ancient boards-and-batten depot in the Athens County hamlet of Canaanville on the Baltimore & Ohio Southwestern Railroad, part of the Baltimore & Ohio system. (Chilcote)

18. In what is unmistakably an original structure and one reminiscent of pioneer facilities in New England, the depot of the Cincinnati, Hamilton & Dayton (Baltimore & Ohio) at College Corner in Preble County reflects its considerable age in this ca. 1910 postcard view. (Chilcote)

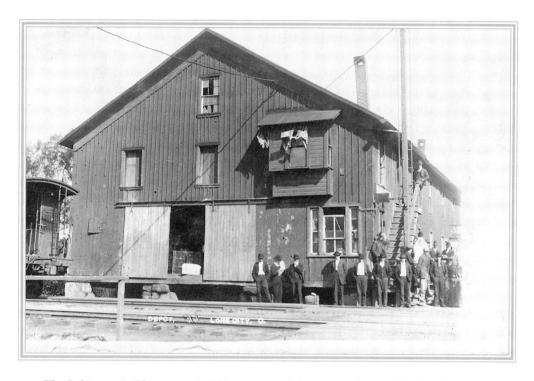

19. The Baltimore & Ohio, an early Ohio carrier and the owner of several local predecessor companies, had a bizarre depot at Lore City in Guernsey County. Surely this structure initially served a nonrailroad function. (Chilcote)

20. A vintage store quartered patrons of the Pennsylvania at Beloit in Columbiana County. The steps from the building to the tracks hindered easy access to trains, especially for shipments of express and freight. (Chilcote)

21. The Erie Railroad selected an ornate style for its depot at Geauga Lake. The second story, located above the agent's office, served as a storage area and not as a tiny apartment. (Chilcote)

22. The Hocking Valley, a property long controlled by the Chesapeake & Ohio and fused into it in 1930, picked an unusual architectural design for its depot at Canal Winchester, southeast of Columbus. (Chilcote)

23. During the picture postcard era, Ohio had two communities named "Valley Junction." One was located in Hamilton County on the Big Four, and the other was in Tuscarawas County. In the latter place, the above image, trains of the Baltimore & Ohio, Pennsylvania, and Wheeling & Lake Erie called at this small union depot, and the public could patronize a convenient privately owned lunch room. (Chilcote)

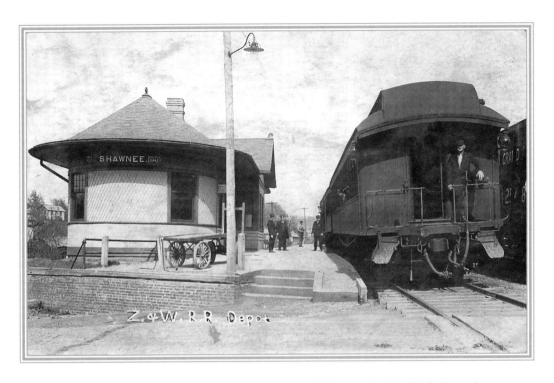

24. The Zanesville & Western Railroad, a corporation folded into the New York Central system in 1922, built an attractive depot at Shawnee with a rounded waiting room. (Chilcote)

25. The Madison County town of West Jefferson possessed a Pennsylvania depot with an unusual configuration. The diagonal alignment may have been dictated by a public road. (Chilcote)

26. Because of its location at the crossing of the east-west main line of the Pennsylvania and the north-south line of affiliate Cleveland, Akron & Columbus, Orrville, in Wayne County, received a strangely shaped depot. This striking structure has been preserved as a museum. (Chilcote)

27. Omega, a station on the Norfolk & Western Railway five miles northeast of Waverly, Pike County, sported a simple boards-and-batten depot with an attractive decorative tower that sliced through the roofline. (Chilcote)

28. A likely older depot, but also one with a tower decoration, served the Norfolk & Western Railway at Kingston, twenty-six miles north of Omega. (Chilcote)

29. Baltimore & Ohio affiliate Baltimore & Ohio Southwestern erected a pleasing Queen Anne–style depot in the village of Madisonville, Hamilton County, in 1888. (Chilcote)

30. Residents of Ada, nearly midway between Pittsburgh and Chicago on the main line of the Pennsylvania, surely appreciated the architectural beauty of their hometown depot. The second floor area may have provided either additional office space or a small apartment. (Chilcote)

31. The Cincinnati Northern Railroad, part of the vibrant New York Central system, constructed a classic Victorian-period depot at Paulding, seat of Paulding County. This 244-mile rail satellite linked Cincinnati with Jackson, Michigan. (Chilcote)

32. While county seat communities had at least a combination depot—a structure with waiting room, center office, and freight-baggage section—smaller towns might possess a scaled-down version. At times these structures had only a waiting room and freight section. A custodian or part-time agent sold tickets, billed freight, and conducted other duties from a desk or counter area. "Union Depot" is the whimsical comment penned on this picture postcard of the New York Central station at Augusta, five miles southeast of Minerva in Carroll County. The card sender noted that the train belonged to the "LEA&W RR." This carrier, the Lake Erie, Alliance & Wheeling, was then operated by the Lake Shore & Michigan Southern, part of the New York Central system. (Chilcote)

33. Holland, a station on the New York Central (Lake Shore & Michigan Southern) ten miles west of Toledo, received barely more than a shelter. The styling resembles a farmer's outbuilding rather than a transportation structure. (Chilcote)

34. Bangs, served by the Pennsylvania's Cleveland, Akron & Columbus, was a hamlet five miles southwest of Mt. Vernon. Yet the Pennsylvania added some architectural detailing to enhance this approximately 10-by-20-foot depot. (Chilcote)

35. The Hocking Valley selected a small building for its Athens County station at Floodwood. A modified hip roof produces a more substantial appearance than the gable roofs that cover the depots at Augusta, Bangs, and Holland. While some of the previously shown depots may have been built from standard designs, the structure at Floodwood surely fits this category. Such carbon-copy plans allowed railroads to construct buildings quickly and cheaply, while still permitting modifications to meet local requirements. If properly conceived, standardized depots could become an architectural corporate logo. (Chilcote)

36. The Wheeling & Lake Erie built a modest depot for its Mogadore station near Akron. (Chilcote)

37. Ney, a farming village in Defiance County, received a typical wooden depot of the Cincinnati Northern. Only a few roof-support brackets break the monotony of this spartan structure. (Chilcote)

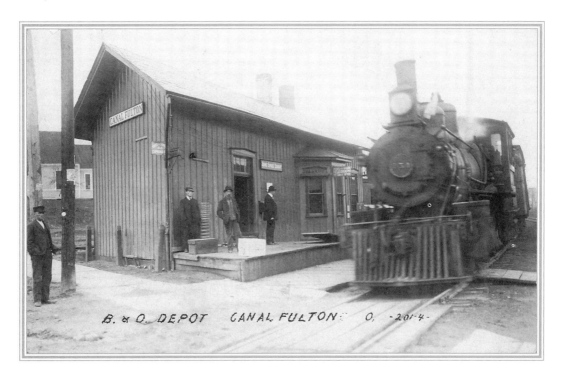

38. The Baltimore & Ohio spent only several hundred dollars for its depot at Canal Fulton in Stark County. (Chilcote)

39. The New York Central system erected a small depot at Paris, a rural station between Alliance and Minerva. Vines have enhanced the visual appeal of this unadorned building. (Chilcote)

40. The quintessential portrait of the country railroad station in Ohio is this 1911 scene of the Northern Ohio Railway depot at Plymouth. (Chilcote)

41. Residents of Warsaw Junction, near Coshocton, a station where two Pennsylvania-affiliated roads crossed, got an architecturally attractive combination depot. The agent and a visitor, a team of horses, dog, milk cans, and a shipment of "Ward's Mother's Bread" make up this view of April 22, 1912. (Chilcote)

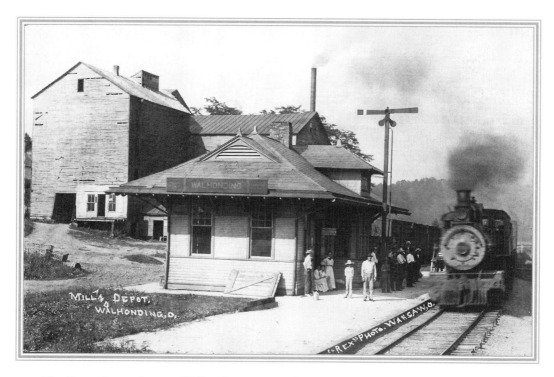

42. The Pennsylvania depot at Walhonding was a carbon copy of the one at Warsaw Junction, eight miles away. Both were located on the 95-mile Dennison-Mansfield branch. (Chilcote)

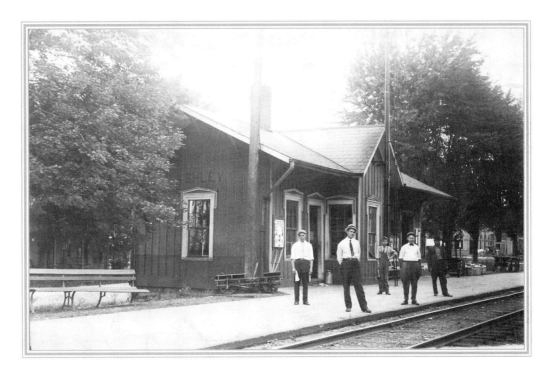

43. The Big Four erected a standard combination depot at Ashley, located between Galion and Delaware on its Cleveland to Columbus main line. (Chilcote)

44. The Chesapeake & Ohio of Indiana, the Chesapeake & Ohio's "New Short Line between Chicago and Cincinnati" completed at the turn of the century, erected a combination depot of standardized styling in the Butler County village of Okeana, twenty-eight miles northwest of Cincinnati. (Chilcote)

45. Small-town combination depots in Ohio and elsewhere usually featured frame construction; only a few were brick. The Pennsylvania selected brick for an unknown reason for its depot at Lucas, seven miles east of Mansfield on its east-west speedway. (Chilcote)

46. Raymond, also spelled Raymond's, received a carbon-copy depot of a popular design employed by New York Central affiliate Toledo & Ohio Central. Raymond is located on the Toledo-Corning, Ohio, main line. As the signboard indicates, this Union County station is 95.7 miles from Toledo and 36.5 miles from Columbus. (Chilcote)

47. The Erie Railroad, popularly dubbed the "Weary Erie" because of its several receiverships, spent modestly on its depot at Burghill, near Cortland on the Shenango, Pennsylvania-Leavittsburg line. The company sold advertising space on depot walls to increase income. (Chilcote)

48. The Baltimore & Ohio put up a small depot of standard design at Bethesda, Belmont County, on its original Washington, D.C. to Chicago line, via Wheeling, West Virginia. (Chilcote)

49. At Madison, located between Ashtabula and Painesville on the main line of the Lake Shore & Michigan Southern, a vital part of the New York Central, the company erected a standard combination depot of frame construction. The metal roof is the only unusual feature. As with numerous stations in Ohio before World War I, a modern water system was lacking. Patrons, including the agent, shared a tin cup at the pump. (Chilcote)

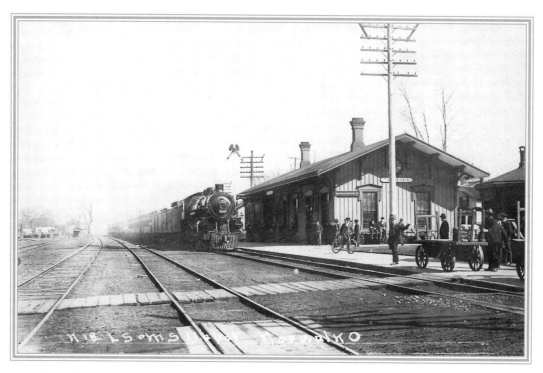

50. Norwalk, situated on a secondary main line of the Lake Shore & Michigan Southern between Elyria and Toledo, possessed an older yet standard depot. This boards-and-batten structure likely dates from the Civil War era. (Chilcote)

51. Lindsey, a station on the Toledo & Ohio Central in Fairfield County, had an inexpensive frame depot. An extended gable roof and barge boards enhanced the modest style. (Chilcote)

52. The Baltimore & Ohio, which built numerous long and narrow frame combination depots along its thirteen-state system, chose one for Chardon, a county seat town on its Niles-Painesville branch. (Chilcote)

53. The Pennsylvania depot at Atwater, a country station on the Cleveland & Pittsburgh Division, resembles the Baltimore & Ohio structure at Chardon, long and narrow. (Chilcote)

54. Residents of Sabina, Clinton County, saw trains of both the Baltimore & Ohio and Pennsylvania systems; in fact, the two stations were only thirty yards apart. The depot in the foreground belonged to the Cincinnati & Muskingum Valley unit of the Pennsylvania and was built to standard plans. (Chilcote)

55. Bremen, located on the Pennsylvania's Cincinnati & Muskingum Valley, received a depot from the same plan book as Sabina. The railroad considered Bremen to be a more important place and therefore the length of the depot is greater. This likely occurred because the Pennsylvania rented space to the Toledo & Ohio Central. A tender of a T&OC freight locomotive can be seen in the left background. (Chilcote)

56. The Fairfield County community of Baltimore possessed an inexpensive Toledo & Ohio Central depot. An extended gable roof and barge boards improve the building's appearance. (Chilcote)

57. A passenger train steams into the "B&O Depot" at Monroeville. Two other steam railroads, Lake Shore & Michigan Southern and Wheeling & Lake Erie, shared this modest frame station. (Chilcote)

58. Tiro, a station seventeen miles northwest of Mansfield on the Pennsylvania's 85-mile Mansfield-Toledo secondary main line, received a small yet functional combination depot. (Chilcote)

59. The Marietta, Columbus & Cleveland Railroad, controlled by the New York Central and known from 1918 to 1952 as the Federal Valley Railroad, connected Marietta and Palos, a distance of forty-five miles. The Amesville depot, situated at milepost 32 (from Marietta) served a coal-mining and farming community. (Chilcote)

60. The depot at Jewett, built by the Pennsylvania and also used by the Wheeling & Lake Erie, served this hilly Harrison County village. (Chilcote)

61. Located six miles south of Steubenville on the Pennsylvania, the depot at Brilliant represents an early standard style. (Chilcote)

62. The Hocking Valley employed a distinctive type of carbon-copy combination depot design. Carey, a Wyandot County trading center, received one of these attractive buildings. (Chilcote)

63. While situated on the Toledo & Ohio Central, the depot at Hatton appears to be built from the same planbook as the Hocking Valley structure at Carey. The hip-gable roof and a hip-gable dormer constitute the dominant architectural features. (Chilcote)

64. Unionville, three miles east of Madison in Lake County, a station on the Lake Shore & Michigan Southern, sported an early standardized combination depot. (Chilcote)

65. In a depot style popular with several Midwestern carriers, the Toledo & Ohio Central erected this combination structure at Marengo in Morrow County. (Chilcote)

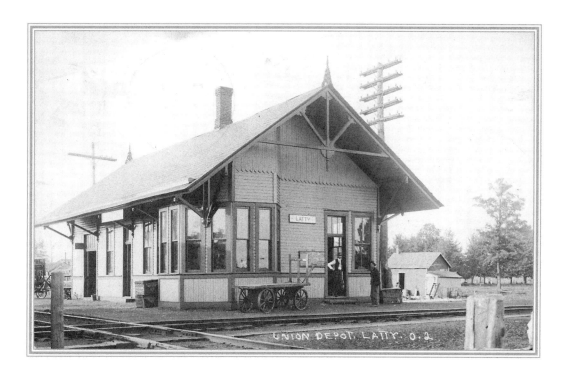

66. The farming village of Latty, Paulding County, claimed a dual or "union" depot. This structure served the Cincinnati Northern and the Nickel Plate roads. The windows of the agent's bay office provided easy viewing of both lines. (Chilcote)

67. A typical Pennsylvania frame combination depot served the community of Kensington, a station between Alliance and Wellsville in Columbiana County. (Chilcote)

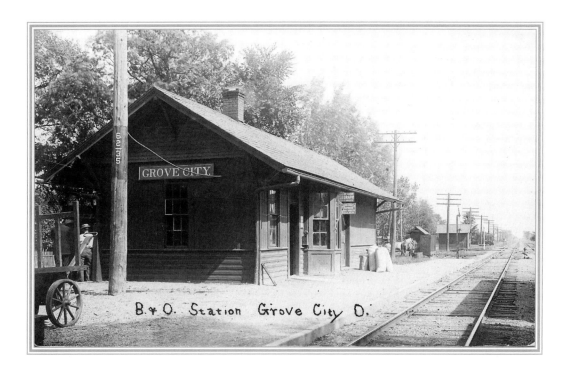

68. Grove City, situated on the Baltimore & Ohio Southwestern, eight miles south of Columbus, received a spartan standard frame combination depot. The dark paint hardly enhances the appearance. (Chilcote)

69. A slightly more attractive depot than the one at Grove City once stood in Spencer. The Wheeling & Lake Erie wisely selected a contrasting paint scheme. (Chilcote)

70. The Pennsylvania picked a standard depot design for its building at Waldo, an agricultural community in Marion County on the Columbus-Sandusky line. (Chilcote)

71. The Cincinnati, Hamilton & Dayton Railroad, which officially joined the Baltimore & Ohio system in 1917, erected a handsome combination depot with a dominant hip roof at Xenia. (Chilcote)

72. Several Ohio railroads regularly opted for hip rather than gable roofs. The Erie was such a carrier. The Richwood depot, on the Dayton-Marion branch, is an example. (Chilcote)

73. The Baltimore & Ohio also favored the hip roof. Its depot at Kent sports this style. Unlike the Richwood building, a tiny roof vent breaks the roof on the south elevation. (Chilcote)

74. The affluent Pennsylvania could afford a substantial brick edifice in Hudson, a busy junction in Summit County. (Chilcote)

75. The Pennsylvania likewise selected brick for its depot at South Charleston, Clark County, a station on the Columbus-Xenia-Cincinnati line. This postcard, mailed on February 16, 1913, shows the depot soon after its completion. Perhaps this smart structure replaced one that had been destroyed by fire or storm. (Chilcote)

MOTIVE POWER AND TRAINS

76. 77. The development of railroad motive power for passenger service is seen in these postcard views of trains in Ashland of the Lorain, Ashland & Southern, a short line that the Pennsylvania controlled

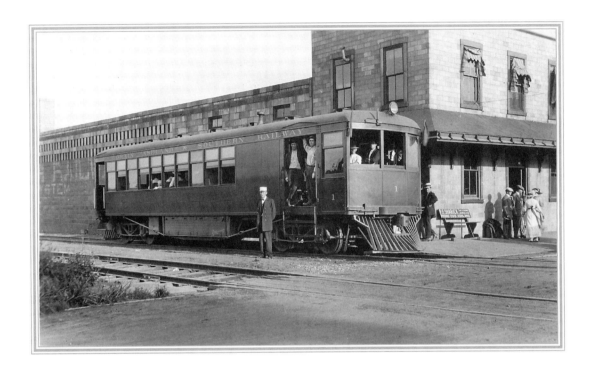

between 1916 and 1921. This woebegone carrier, which linked Lorain and Custaloga, sixty-seven miles, found that an internal combustion motor car was cheaper to operate than a conventional steam train. (Chilcote)

78. The Bellefontaine (Ohio) Art Company sold this picture postcard of "Fat Annie," a powerful Pacific-type (4-6-2) steam locomotive of the Pennsylvania Railroad. Railroaders picked the "Fat Annie" nickname for this Class K28 Pacific because the boiler was much larger ("fatter") than the one of the Atlantic type (4-4-2) that it replaced. (Delap)

79. An inspection locomotive, pulling two business cars, speeds along the Ohio main line of the New York Central. (Chilcote)

80. A Wheeling & Lake Erie locomotive is being turned at the engine house at Justus, near Brewster in Stark County, about 1909. (Delap)

81. Two passenger trains wait at the Thurston depot. While one line belongs to the Toledo & Ohio Central and the other to the Zanesville & Western, the New York Central controlled both carriers. (Chilcote)

BIG FOUR Limited, Mechanicsburg, Ohio.

82. The "Big Four Limited," a highly exaggerated moniker, stops at the Mechanicsburg station early in the century. An American Standard (4-4-0) engine, a popular passenger locomotive, smokes heavily. The engineer apparently did not believe that "smoke is fuel wasted." (Chilcote)

83. An eastbound freight and a westbound passenger stand in the Cumberland station of the 112-mile Ohio River & Western Railway, which connected Bellaire and Zanesville. The Pennsylvania controlled this cheaply built narrow-gauge pike after 1912. (Chilcote)

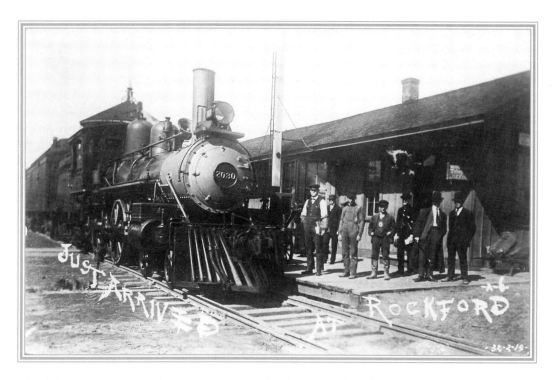

84. A high-stepping 4-4-0 American locomotive has "just arrived" at the Cincinnati Northern station at Rockford in Mercer County. (Chilcote)

85. A freight train awaits orders at the Bristolville station (residents called the village Bristol), near Niles on the Pennsylvania's Ashtabula to Youngstown line. The locomotive sports an oil headlight instead of a modern electric one. (Chilcote)

N.Y.C.R.R. - Tr. No. 624 passing Shawville Station, 7-23-15

86. A New York Central passenger train blasts through the village of Shawville between Cleveland and Elyria in the summer of 1915. (Chilcote)

Erie Depot and Train No. 16, North Lewisburg, Ohio.

87. A ten-wheeler, used for both freight and passenger service, pauses at the Erie station in North Lewisburg, pulling the daily northbound No. 16 from Cincinnati to Youngstown. Train time is 11:30 a.m. (Chilcote)

88. The fireman takes off a few moments to watch the activities at the Wheeling & Lake Erie station at Valley Junction. The locomotive, No. 350, has the popular 4-4-0 wheel arrangement. (Chilcote)

89. A sister locomotive, No. 354, pulls the "fast train" on the Wheeling & Lake Erie into the Adena station. This coal-mining center is in Jefferson County. (Chilcote)

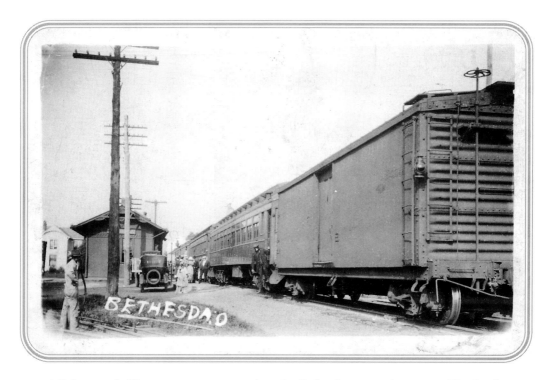

90. A Baltimore & Ohio passenger train stands at the Bethesda station about 1920. The freight car on the end is for hauling less-than-carload freight. Railroaders often called this the "peddler car." (Chilcote)

photo by Gorsuch. Elkton Bridge, 104 Feet High, Lisbon, Ohio.

THE RAILROAD CORRIDOR

91. A. C. Gorsuch, a Lisbon commercial photographer, captured a Pittsburgh, Lisbon & Western passenger train crossing the imposing S-curve bridge near Elkton, east of Lisbon, about 1909. Graffiti adorns the bridge. (Delap)

B. & O. TRESTLE CROSSING PENN'A R. R., WOOSTER, O.

92. A steel bridge and wooden trestle with scores of bents allowed the Lodi-Millersburg branch of the Baltimore & Ohio to cross the main line of the Pennsylvania near Wooster. (Delap)

93. The railroad corridor along the Baltimore & Ohio at Piedmont, Harrison County, which includes a "handle factory," is shown in this 1908 view card. (Chilcote)

94. The yards of the Wheeling & Lake Erie, probably at Dillonvale near Martins Ferry, are crowded with loaded cars of coal. (Delap)

95. A New York Central locomotive moves about the gritty yards at Ashtabula Harbor. The card owner made this notation on the reverse side: "This is a Small portion of our Union Docks." (Delap)

96. The rural Clemons station of the Toledo & Ohio Central in Licking County is highlighted by a large water tank. (Chilcote)

97. The Belmont County hamlet of Pittsburg, a station on the Ohio River & Western narrow-gauge, is largely a cluster of houses and a school near the simple depot building. (Chilcote)

98. The tracks and depots of the Big Four and Erie railroads slice the commercial heart of Osborn near Dayton. The Erie spelled the community with a final "e." (Chilcote)

99. Railroad facilities, including the depot and water tank of the Toledo & Ohio Central, are depicted in this panoramic view of Rushville in Fairfield County. (Chilcote)

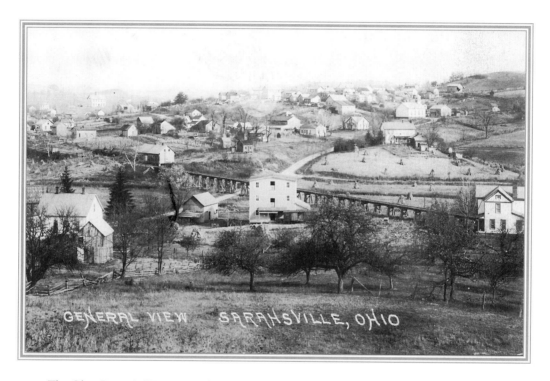

100. The Ohio River & Western tracks cut through the rough terrain of the Noble County village of Sarahsville. The small frame depot is in the left portion of the picture. A flour mill, with boxcar spotted nearby, is in the foreground. (Chilcote)

101. The clutter of the Ohio River & Western station area in Summerfield, a Noble County village approximately midway between the terminals of Bellaire and Zanesville, is fully revealed. The road's battered engine house and turntable appear in the right-hand portion of this postcard view. (Chilcote)

102. The depot and tower (right) of the Erie and Wheeling & Lake Erie crossing at Creston in Wayne County are typical of a busy part of the Ohio railway corridor. The double-track line belongs to the Erie. (Chilcote)

103. Communities occasionally claimed a "depot park," which was probably railroad owned and maintained. The "RR Park" at Orrville, north of the Pennsylvania depot, contained a Civil War cannon. (Delap)

104. 105. Floods periodically ravaged the railroad corridor in Ohio, as they did during Easter week 1913. Nearly every river community experienced severe flooding; indeed, this deluge of water produced

the state's greatest natural disaster. The Sandusky River swamps the Wheeling & Lake Erie station at Fremont. (104) The Mahoning River closes the Pennsylvania station at Warren. (105) (both Chilcote)

OHIOANS AND RAILROADS

106. The product of a postcard camera, "AMHERST OR BUST" shows what is probably a father and son on a railroad velocipede. The message to Charles Krneck in Elyria reads: "Dear Cousin. So you think we will ever land if we don't go any faster than we are going now. We will land but god only knows where." (Delap)

107. Railroad workers, joined by curious onlookers, gather at trackside in Creston to assist a "big hook" clearing a derailment. (Delap)

108. Another wreck, which occurred in August 1909 on the Northern Ohio Railway near Spencer, likewise drew a mix of laborers and bystanders. (Delap)

109. A bridge construction crew caught the attention of a cardmaker near Magrew on the Pennsylvania's Panhandle Division. (Delap)

110. Railroad workers (right) and possibly two visitors stand near a shanty, identified on the back of the card as "The Hump, Wellington, O." (Delap)

111. A large group of laborers, possibly assigned to maintenance-of-way duties, gathers by the tower at the crossing of the Cincinnati, Hamilton & Dayton and Nickel Plate at Leipsic Junction. (Chilcote)

112. A section crew poses for the camera at the Lock 17 depot of the Pennsylvania between Gnadenhutten and Port Washington in Tuscarawas County in 1908. (Chilcote)

113. The agent for the Wheeling & Lake Erie (controlled by George Gould's Wabash Railway) joins local section hands at the Zoar station. (Delap)

114. Members of a track gang of the Pennsylvania, most with "No. 2" shovels, pause from their work assignments at Austinburg in Ashtabula County. (Chilcote)

115. A train crew (conductor, third from left) stands near the New York Central depot at Kinsman on the Ashtabula-Youngstown line. (Chilcote)

116. This unusual railroad photocard features an insert of the Toledo & Ohio Central station agent at Cygnet in Wood County. (Chilcote)

117. These members of the depot force at DeGraff, Logan County, a station on the Big Four, proudly reveal that they are union men, belonging to the Order of Railroad Telegraphers. (Chilcote)

118. Workers, including perhaps the agent at Stockport, a station on the Marietta to Zanesville line (Ohio & Little Kanawha Railway) of the Baltimore & Ohio, literally roll out the barrels. (Chilcote)

119. Two section workers, employed by either the Erie or New York Central, pose with their foreman, A. F. Garver (left), at Martel in Marion County. (Delap)

120. A train crew, conductor and brakemen, please a photographer by the caboose of a Baltimore & Ohio freight train. The location, noted on the message side, is given as "e. of Newark, Oh." (Delap)

121. This real-photo card, presumably taken in the Hocking Valley yards of Columbus in 1909, says, in part: "Here is that picture I promised you. Ain't it a dandy." (Delap)

122. A Baltimore & Ohio construction gang takes time for its picture in front of a string of bunk cars. The exact location is unknown. (Delap)

123. Employees of the Cincinnati Northern are building a water tank north of Paulding, perhaps along the Maumee River. (Delap)

124. It must be nearly train time on June 27, 1913, at the Baltimore & Ohio station at Warwick near Akron. A variety of passengers, greeters, and loafers congregate. Even a dog joins the group. Empty bread boxes await their return to the Akron Baking Company. (Chilcote)

125. An unusually large crowd of adults, dressed in their Sunday best, wait on the platform of the Wabash depot at Antwerp in Paulding County. (Chilcote)

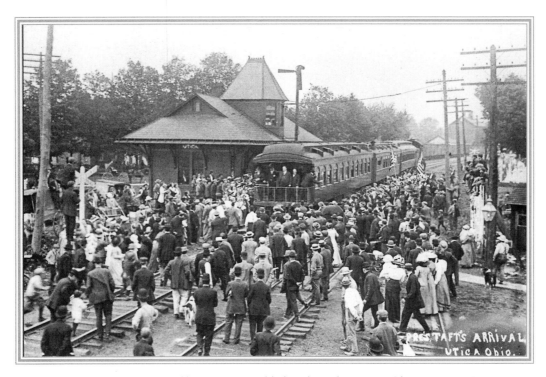

126. The reason for the mass of humanity assembled at the Baltimore & Ohio station in Utica is to greet Ohio's native son, President William Howard Taft. (Delap)

127. On a wintry day in Cleveland, a crowd meets a train on the Erie Railroad at the East 55th Street station. Perhaps the event is the send-off of men to serve in World War I. (Chilcote)

128. "Off for Grocers Picnic" was surely an event that highlighted the summer of 1909 for some residents of western Ohio. (Chilcote)

129. A relief train for flood victims drew a substantial crowd to the College Corner station in March 1913. (Delap)

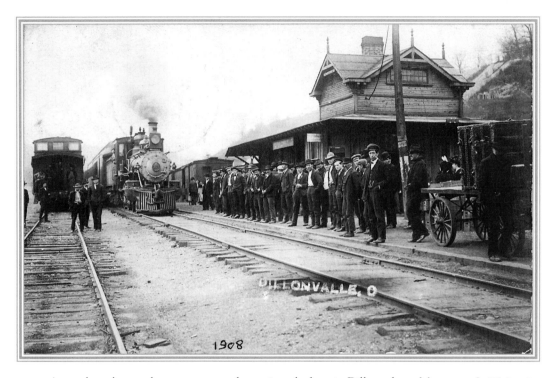

130. A mostly male crowd congregates on the station platform in Dillonvale on May 4, 1908. (Chilcote)

131. A small group of happy females stands near the Cincinnati Northern depot in West Alexandria, west of Dayton. (Grant)

132. This novelty card, mailed from East Liverpool in February 1913, surely tickled the funny bones of both sender and receiver. (Delap)

133. A commercial photographer catches a man "leaving" Akron on an imaginary train. This type of personalized image was a popular part of the picture postcard age. (Grant)

OHIO'S RAILWAY AGE  IN POSTCARDS

ELECTRIC

ROLLING STOCK

1. In this classic scene near Sandusky, presumably staged by the Lake Shore Electric Railway, an interurban car passes over the *Lake Shore & Michigan Southern Limited*, a crack train of the New York Central system. (Chilcote)

2. A New Philadelphia postcard firm, "Green's Famous Post Cards," issued this real-photo view of a Northern Ohio Traction & Light Company interurban car near the Stark County village of Beach City. (Chilcote)

3. Two electric cars of the Stark Electric Railway meet at the Damascus station about 1910. Car no. 4 is headed to Salem, the eastern terminus, and car no. 2 is bound for Canton, the western terminus. This 33-mile road, which opened in 1903, survived until 1939. (Chilcote)

4. A heavy-weight wooden car of the Toledo & Western Railway waits at the Fayette station early in the century. This Toledo-based interurban planned to connect with the electric roads of Indiana, but it never extended further west then Pioneer, in northern Williams County. (Chilcote)

5. A car of the Lake Shore Electric Railway has just arrived at its storefront depot in Huron. Express shipments are being "worked" and a "drummer" (salesman), bags in hand, leaves the trackside area. (Chilcote)

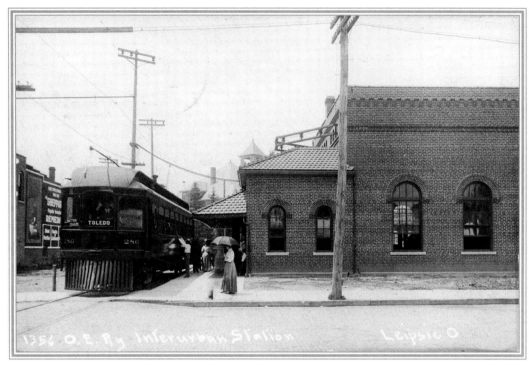

6. Ohio's largest interurban, the Ohio Electric Railway, owned a sizable combination brick depot and electrical substation at Leipsic. This Putnam County community, located on the company's Lima-Toledo Division, was twenty-six miles from Lima and forty-six miles from Toledo. (Chilcote)

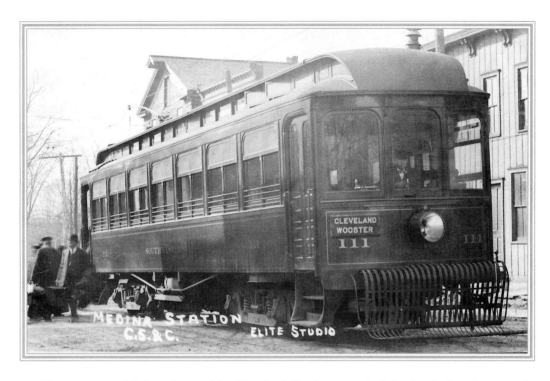

7. It's train time at Medina. A car of the Cleveland, Southwestern & Columbus Railway has arrived in this county seat community. From the signboard, No. 111 was assigned to the Cleveland-Wooster route rather than Cleveland-Bucyrus service. (Chilcote)

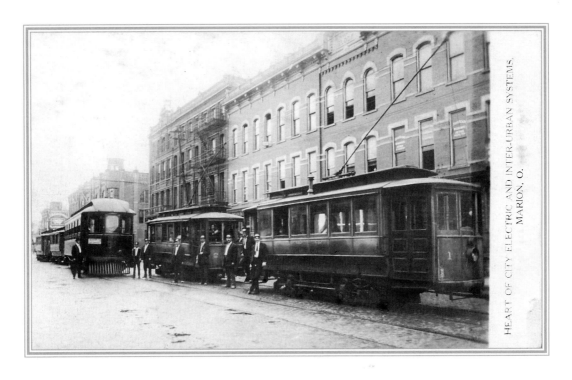

8. C. G. Waint Bookseller and Stationer in Marion sold this card picturing the interurban equipment of the fifty-mile Columbus, Delaware & Marion Railway *(left)* and the local street railway company *(right)*. (Chilcote)

9. A professional cardmaker caught a car of the Youngstown & Ohio River Railroad along its 36-mile Salem to East Liverpool route. (Chilcote)

10. An interurban car of Cleveland, Southwestern & Columbus (later Cleveland & Southwestern) rumbles over a city street in downtown Ashland. The Ashland Drug Company marketed this postcard. (Chilcote)

11. Wrecks occasionally plagued interurbans. A cardmaker likely quickly created and sold this scene of a derailed Lake Shore Electric car at Rocky River west of Cleveland. (Chilcote)

THE INTERURBAN CORRIDOR

12. A construction train, steam-powered, rattles along a downtown Ashland street during the building of the Cleveland, Columbus & Southwestern Railway between Seville and Mansfield in 1908. (Chilcote)

13. This unidentified real-photo card of a depot-substation probably belonged to the Ohio Electric Railway. (Chilcote)

14. The Scioto Valley Traction Company, the only Ohio interurban that used a "third rail" for portions of its operations, constructed a substantial brick-and-tile station at Canal Winchester. (Grant)

15. This view of the Lake Shore Electric power plant at Beach Park, seven miles east of Lorain, reveals the massive financial investments that capitalists made in one of America's most important interurbans. (Chilcote)

16. The interurban corridor, including track, overhead wire, and station *(left)*, is shown at New Bremen in Shelby County. The Western Ohio Railway served this farming community. (Chilcote)

17. One of Ohio's obscure interurbans, the Wellston & Jackson Belt Railway, opened in 1896 between Jackson and Wellston (eighteen miles) through a coal-mining section of Jackson County. The interurban, which the steam Hocking Valley Railroad owned, shared its Jackson station with its parent firm. The Wellston & Jackson Belt gained the dubious distinction of being one of the first Midwestern interurbans to close; scrappers removed the rails, ties, poles, and wire in 1915. (Chilcote)

18. Interurbans in Ohio and the Midwest commonly constructed brick facilities because of the threat of electric fires. The Stark Electric Railway erected this three-stall masonry carbarn in Alliance at the turn of the century. (Chilcote)

19. The "Interurban Station" in Delaware consisted of a storefront office on a principal street. Likely both the Columbus, Delaware & Marion and Columbus, Magnetic Springs & Northern railways used this depot. (Chilcote)

20. Residents of Archbold, Fulton County, patronized an unusual interurban facility. The Toledo & Indiana Railway, which linked Toledo and Bryan, fifty-six miles, shared a building with town government. (Grant)

21. An early Ohio interurban was the Cleveland, Painesville & Eastern Railroad, which opened its core line on July 4, 1896. The company subsequently expanded, including an extension from Painesville to Ashtabula. Willoughby emerged as the center of operations, with this complex of station, office, carbarn, and repair facilities. (Chilcote)

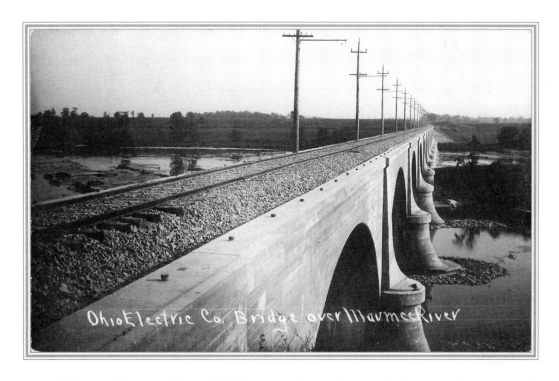

22. While interurbans typically installed cheap, wooden trestles, some bridges were of concrete and steel. An illustration of an expensive bridge was this one over the Maumee River that belonged to the Ohio Electric Railway. (Chilcote)

23. Similarly, the Cleveland, Painesville & Eastern constructed an elaborate metal bridge at Willoughby. The controlling Everett-Moore interests, powerful interurban developers, could finance such an impressive structure. (Chilcote)

24. The Toledo, Port Clinton & Lakeside Railway, which connected Toledo, Port Clinton, and Marblehead, owned a three-mile line between Marblehead and a pier at Bay Point from which an independent operator provided steamer service on Lake Erie to Cedar Point and Sandusky. (Chilcote)

OHIO'S RAILWAY AGE  IN POSTCARDS

REFERENCE MATERIAL

NOTES

1. Harry N. Scheiber, *Ohio Canal Era: A Case Study of Government and the Economy, 1820–1861* (Athens, Ohio: Ohio University Press, 1969).

2. Clipping (1859), *Erie Railroad Employee's Magazine* file, Erie Lackawanna Railway papers, The University of Akron Archives, Akron, Ohio.

3. Walter Rumsey Marvin, "Columbus and the Railroads of Central Ohio before the Civil War" (unpublished doctoral dissertation, Ohio State University, 1953), 12; Walter Rumsey Marvin, "The Steubenville and Indiana Railroad: The Pennsylvania's Middle Route To the Middle West," *The Ohio Historical Quarterly* 66 (January 1957): 12; R. S. Kayler, "Ohio Railroads," *Ohio Archaeological and Historical Society Publications* 9 (1901): 189; John F. Stover, *Iron Road to the West: American Railroads in the 1850's* (New York: Columbia University Press, 1978), 13.

4. Charles Ambler, *History of Transportation in the Ohio Valley* (Glendale, Calif.: Arthur H. Clark Co., 1932); Andrew M. Modelski, *Railroad Maps of North America: The First Hundred Years* (Washington, D.C.: Library of Congress, 1984), 75.

5. John J. George, Jr., "The Miami Canal," *Ohio Archaeological and Historical Society Publications* 36 (1927): 109–10; David H. Mould, *Dividing Lines: Canals, Railroads and Urban Rivalry in Ohio's Hocking Valley, 1825–1875* (Dayton, Ohio: Wright State University Press, 1994), 81.

6. Stover, *Iron Road to the West*, 13, 115–16, 122–36.

7. Alfred D. Chandler, Jr., *The Visible Hand: The Managerial Revolution in American Business* (Cambridge, Mass.: Harvard University Press, 1977), 145–87.

8. H. Roger Grant, *Erie Lackawanna: Death of an American Railroad, 1938–1992* (Stanford, Calif.: Stanford University Press, 1994), 6; George H. Minor, *The Erie System: The Organization and Corporate History* (Cleveland: Erie Railroad Company, 1936), 67–80, 375–76.

9. *Poor's Manual of the Railroads of the United States* (New York: H.V. & H.W. Poor, 1902), 320–21.

10. H. Roger Grant, *Land, Air, Water: Transportation and Ohio* (Columbus, Ohio: The State Library of Ohio, 1979), 11; H. Roger Grant, "Land Development in the Middle West: The Case of the Akron, Canton & Youngstown Railroad, 1913–1925," *The Old Northwest* 1 (December 1975): 359, 361–62, 368–69.

11. *Statistics of Railways in the United States* (Washington, D.C.: Interstate Commerce Commission, 1934), 4; *Yearbook of Railroad Information* (New York: Committee on Public Relations of the Eastern Railroads, 1936), 3.

12. "Right-of-Way," 16-mm film produced by the Office of War Information, 1943, National Archives, Washington, D.C.; *Historical Statistics of the United States: Colonial Times to 1957* (Washington, D.C.: U.S. Department of Commerce, 1960), 427, 430–31.

13. Maury Klein, *Unfinished Business: The Railroad in American Life* (Hanover, N.H.: University Press of New England, 1994), 143–65.

14. "Capitol Limited," brochure, Baltimore & Ohio Railroad, 1949.

15. William F. Howes, Jr., interview by author, Williamsport, Pennsylvania, September 29, 1994.

16. Grant, *Land, Air, Water*, 12; Grant, *Erie Lackawanna*, 208–9, 212.

17. Jerry Jacobson, interview by author, Akron, Ohio, December 2, 1994.

18. "Ohio Rail Map," Ohio Department of Transportation, 1995.

19. *Ohio Statesman* (Columbus, Ohio), June 13, 1850.

20. See H. Roger Grant and Charles W. Bohi, *The Country Railroad Station in America* (Boulder, Colo.: Pruett Publishing Co., 1978), 3–10.

21. John F. Stover, *History of the Baltimore and Ohio Railroad* (West Lafayette, Ind.: Purdue University Press, 1987), 152, 156.

22. Grant, *Erie Lackawanna*, 9; B.A. Botkin and Alvin F. Harlow, *A Treasury of Railroad Folklore* (New York: Crown Publishers, 1953), 500–505; Norris F. Schneider, *Bent, Zigzag and Crooked: Ohio's Last Narrow Gauge Railroad* (Zanesville, Ohio: By the Author, 1960).

23. John Vander Mass collection, Special Collections Department, University of Iowa Libraries, Iowa City, Iowa.

24. E.L. Doctorow, *Ragtime* (New York: Random House, 1975), 80.

25. George H. Gibson, "High-Speed Electric Interurban Railways," *Annual Report of the Board of Regents of the Smithsonian Institution* (Washington, D.C.: Smithsonian Institution, 1904), 311; George W. Hilton and John F. Due, *The Electric Interurban Railways in America* (Stanford, Calif.: Stanford University Press, 1960), 3, 186–87.

26. Charles B. Clark, "Electric Roads for Rural Districts," *The Breeder's Gazette* 22 (August 24, 1892): 115; "The Farmer and the Interurban," *Street Railway Journal* 28 (October 6, 1906): 497; Guy Morrison Walker, *The Why and How of Interurban Railways* (Chicago: Kenfield Publishing Co., 1904), 3–4; Hilton and Due, *The Electric Interurban Railways in America*, 8.

27. H. Roger Grant, "Interurban!" *Timeline* 3 (April–May 1986): 17; Hilton and Due, *The Electric Interurban Railways in America*, 273.

28. Grant, "Interurban!" 20–21; Stephen D. Hambley, "The Vanguard of a Regional Infrastructure: Electric Railways of Northeast Ohio, 1884–1932" (unpublished doctoral dissertation, The University of Akron, 1993), 80–89.

29. "Completion of Important Link Connecting the Interurban Lines of Ohio, Indiana and Michigan," *Street Railway Journal* 27 (January 6, 1906): 30–31.

30. H. Roger Grant, ed., *We Took the Train* (DeKalb, Ill.: Northern Illinois University Press, 1990), 98–101.

31. Hilton and Due, *The Electric Interurban Railways in America*, 108–12.

32. *Ibid.*, 44, 273; Grant, "Interurban!" 23.

33. Hilton and Due, *The Electric Interurban Railways in America*, 35, 43, 270.

34. Grant, "Interurban!" 26–27, 33; Hilton and Due, *The Electric Interurban Railways in America*, 206, 270; Toledo, Fostoria & Findlay Railway public timetable, October 20, 1929.

35. Northwestern Ohio Railway & Power Company public

timetable, June 27, 1915; Hambley, "The Vanguard of a Regional Infrastructure," 399–441.

36. George W. Hilton, "The Wrong Track," *Invention & Technology* (Spring 1993): 47–54.

37. John Walker Harrington, "Postal Carditis and Some Allied Manias," *American Illustrated Magazine* 61 (March 1906): 562–67; George Miller and Dorothy Miller, *Picture Postcards in the United States, 1893–1918* (New York: Clarkson N. Potter, 1976), 20–21; Ray D. Applegate, *Trolleys and Streetcars on American Picture Postcards* (New York: Dover, 1979), v.

38. *Annual Report of the Commissioner of Railroads and Telegraphs* [1887] (Columbus, Ohio: State Printer, 1888), 29; H. Roger Grant, *Railroad Postcards in the Age of Steam* (Iowa City, Iowa: University of Iowa Press, 1994), 9–10.

39. See John W. Ripley, "The Art of Postcard Fakery," *Kansas Historical Quarterly* 38 (Summer 1972): 124–31; George N. Johnson, Jr., telephone interview by author, Lexington, Virginia, November 21, 1993.

40. Louis W. Goodwin, interview by author, Northfield, Connecticut, May 16, 1992.

41. Hal Morgan and Andreas Brown, *Prairie Fires and Paper Moons: The American Photographic Postcard, 1900–1920* (Boston: David R. Godine, 1981), xiii–xiv; Johnson, interview.

42. Grant, *Railroad Postcards in the Age of Steam*, 4–6.

43. Picture postcard in possession of author.

44. Grant, *Railroad Postcards in the Age of Steam*, 7–8.

45. Johnson, interview.

INDEX

Ada, Ohio, 62
Adena, Ohio, 121
Adrian, Michigan, 4
Akron, Ohio, 7, 9, 17, 165
Akron Baking Company, 156
Akron, Bedford & Cleveland Railroad, 17. *See also* Northern Ohio Traction and Light Company
Akron, Canton & Youngstown Railroad, 7, 8. *See also* Northern Ohio Railway
Alliance, Ohio, 186
Amesville, Ohio, 91
Amherst, Ohio, 138
Amtrak. *See* National Railroad Passenger Corporation
Antwerp, Ohio, 157
Archbold, Ohio, 188
Ashland, Ohio, 108–09, 178, 180
Ashley, Ohio, 75
Ashtabula, Ohio, 127
Atlantic & Great Western Railway, 5
Atwater, Ohio, 85
Augusta, Ohio, 64
Austinburg, Ohio, 146

Baltimore, Ohio, 88
Baltimore & Ohio Railroad, 5, 9, 10, 12, 33, 42–43, 45, 47–48, 51, 55, 70, 80, 84, 86 ,89, 105, 122, 124–25, 152, 154, 156, 158. *See also* Baltimore & Ohio Southwestern Railroad; Cincinnati, Hamilton & Dayton Railway; Ohio & Little Kanawha Railway
Baltimore & Ohio Southwestern Railroad, 49, 61, 100
Bangs, Ohio, 66
Beach City, Ohio, 170
Beach Park, Ohio, 183
Bellaire, Ohio, 40
Bellaire, Zanesville & Cincinnati Railroad, 13. *See also* Ohio River & Western Railway
Beloit, Ohio, 52
Bethesda, Ohio, 80, 122
Big Four Railroad. *See* Cleveland, Cincinnati, Chicago & St. Louis Railroad
Bremen, Ohio, 87
Brilliant, Ohio, 93
Bristolville, Ohio, 117
Burghill, Ohio, 79

Canaanville, Ohio, 49
Canal Fulton, Ohio, 70
Canal Winchester, Ohio, 54, 182
Canton, Ohio, 7
Capitol Limited (passenger train), 9
Carey, Ohio, 94
Central Electric Railway Association, 20
Chardon, Ohio, 84
Chesapeake & Ohio Railway, 45, 76. *See also* Hocking Valley Railway
Chicago & Atlantic Railway, 7
Chicago Junction, Ohio. *See* Willard, Ohio
Cincinnati, Ohio, 7, 28, 36–37
Cincinnati, Hamilton & Dayton Railway, 50, 103, 143, 161
Cincinnati Northern Railroad, 63, 69, 98, 116, 155, 163
Clemons, Ohio, 128
Cleveland, Ohio, 7, 17, 20, 28, 38, 159
Cleveland & Mahoning Valley Railroad, 7
Cleveland, Akron & Columbus Railway, 58, 66

199

Cleveland, Cincinnati, Chicago & St. Louis Railroad, 39, 55, 75, 114, 130, 149
Cleveland, Painesville & Eastern Railroad, 20, 189, 191
Cleveland, Southwestern & Columbus Railway, 175, 178, 180
Coshocton, Ohio, 26
College Corner, Ohio, 50, 161
Columbus, Ohio, 11, 33–34, 153
Columbus & Ohio River Railroad, 11
Columbus & Xenia Rail Road, 11–12
Columbus, Delaware & Marion Railway, 176, 187
Columbus, Magnetic Springs & Northern Railway, 22–23, 187
Conneaut, Ohio, 19
Conneaut & Erie Traction Company, 19
Consolidated Rail Corporation (Conrail), 10–11
Crestline, Ohio, 39
Creston, Ohio, 134, 139
CSX Corporation, 11
Cumberland, Ohio, 115
Cygnet, Ohio, 148

Damascus, Ohio, 171
Dayton, Ohio, 7, 35
De Graff, Ohio, 149
Delaware, Ohio, 22, 187
Delphos, Ohio, 8
Dillonvale, Ohio, 126, 162
Doctorow, E.L., 15

East Liverpool, Ohio, 164
Eastman Kodak Company, 27

Electric interurban railways. *See* Ohio transportation
Elkton, Ohio, 123
Erie Railroad, 5, 7, 13, 41, 53, 79, 104, 119, 130, 134, 151, 159
Erie & Kalamazoo Rail Road, 4
Erie Lackawanna Railway, 10

Fairlawn, Ohio, 8
"Fat Annie" (steam locomotive), 110
Fayette, Ohio, 172
Federal Valley Railroad. See Marietta, Columbus & Cleveland Railroad
Findlay, Ohio, 19
Floodwood, Ohio, 67
Fort Wayne, Indiana, 20
Fostoria, Ohio, 22
Fredericktown, Ohio, 22
Fremont, Ohio, 136

Galion, Ohio, 22
Galion Southern Railway, 22
Geauga Lake, Ohio, 53
Goodyear Tire & Rubber Company, 7
Gorsuch, A.C., 123
Graham, Anderson, Probst & White (architectural firm), 38
Granville, Ohio, 17
Greenwich, Ohio, 47
"Grocers' Picnic," 160
Grove City, Ohio, 100

Hatton, Ohio, 95
Hocking Valley Railway, 33, 54, 67, 94, 153, 185
Holland, Ohio, 65

Hudson, Ohio, 106
Huron, Ohio, 173

Interborough Rapid Transit Company, 19

Jackson, Ohio, 185
Jewett, Ohio, 92
Justus, Ohio, 112

Kensington, Ohio, 99
Kent, Ohio, 41, 105
Kingston, Ohio, 60
Kinsman, Ohio, 147

Lake Erie, 192
Lake Erie & Western Railroad, 13
Lake Erie, Alliance & Wheeling Railroad, 64
Lake Shore & Michigan Southern Limited (passenger train), 169
Lake Shore & Michigan Southern Railroad, 65, 81–82, 89, 96, 169
Lake Shore Electric Railway, 20, 169, 173, 179, 183
Latty, Ohio, 98
Leipsic, Ohio, 174
Leipsic Junction, Ohio, 143
Lima, Ohio, 7, 19–20
Lindsey, Ohio, 83
Lisbon, Ohio, 123
Lock Seventeen, Ohio, 144
Logan, Ohio, 5
Lorain, Ashland & Southern Railroad, 108–09
Lore City, Ohio, 51

Louisville & Nashville Railroad, 36
Lucus, Ohio, 77

Mad River & Lake Erie Railroad, 4
Madison, Ohio, 81
Madisonville, Ohio 61
Magnetic Springs, Ohio, 22–23
Magrew, Ohio, 141
Manhattan Limited (passenger train), 20
Mansfield, Ohio, 7
Marengo, Ohio, 97
Marietta, Columbus & Cleveland Railroad, 91
Marion, Ohio, 7, 22, 176
Martel, Ohio, 151
Maumee River, 190
Mechanicsburg, Ohio, 114
Medina, Ohio, 175
Miami & Erie Canal, 3, 5
Mogadore, Ohio, 68
Monroeville, Ohio, 4, 89
Morrow, Ohio, 13
Moulton, J.S., 19–20

National Railroad Passenger Corportion (Amtrak), 9
New Bremen, Ohio, 184
New York Central System, 5, 13, 71, 111, 118, 127, 147, 151. *See also* Cincinnati Northern Railroad; Lake Erie, Alliance & Wheeling Railroad; Lake Shore & Michigan Southern Railroad
New York, Chicago & St. Louis Railroad, 7, 98, 143

Newark, Ohio, 17, 42, 152
Ney, Ohio, 69
Nickel Plate Road. *See* New York, Chicago & St. Louis Railroad
Norfolk & Western Railway, 33, 36, 45, 59, 60
Norfolk Southern Corporation, 11
North Lewisberg, Ohio, 119
Northern Ohio Railway, 7–8, 72, 140
Northern Ohio Traction & Light Company, 22, 170
Northwestern Ohio Railway & Power Company, 23–24
Norwalk, Ohio, 82

Ohio & Erie Canal, 3–4
Ohio & Little Kanawha Railway, 150
Ohio & Pennsylvania Railroad, 11
Ohio Canal & Steubenville Railway, 4
Ohio Central Railroad, 10–11
Ohio Electric Railway, 20–21, 174, 181, 190
Ohio Interurban Railway Association, 20
Ohio Rail Transportation Authority, 10
Ohio River & Western Railway, 115, 129, 132–33. *See also* Bellaire, Zanesville & Cincinnati Railroad
Ohio transportation: Decline of interurbans, 22–24; depots, 25–26; dieselization, 8–9; early transport forms, 3–5; extent of interurbans, 15, 17, 19–20, 22; interurban freight, 23; maps, 6, 18; popularity of interurbans, 16; railroad development, 4–5, 7–11; social aspects of railroads, 11–13; significance of interurbans, 23
Okeana, Ohio, 76
Omega, Ohio, 59
Order of Railroad Telegraphers, 149
Orrville, Ohio, 58, 135
Osborn, Ohio, 130

Painesville, Ohio, 20
Paris, Ohio, 71
Paulding, Ohio, 63, 155
Penn Central Transportation Company, 10
Pennsylvania Railroad System, 5, 10, 13, 20, 33, 36, 39–40, 44, 46, 52, 55, 58, 62, 73–74, 77, 85–87, 90, 92–93, 99, 102, 106–07, 110, 117, 124, 135, 137, 141, 144, 146. *See also* Cleveland, Akron & Columbus Railway
Pennsylvania & Ohio Railway, 19
Piedmont, Ohio, 125
Pittsburg, Ohio, 129
Pittsburgh, Fort Wayne & Chicago Railroad, 13
Pittsburgh, Lisbon & Western Railroad, 123
Plymouth, Ohio, 72
Portsmouth, Ohio, 45
Postcards, picture: Decline, 28–29; development, 25, 27; marketing, 26–27; popularity, 25, 27–28; practicality, 28; railroad subjects, 25–26, 29; types, 27

Ragtime (novel), 15
Raymond, Ohio, 78

Richmond, Virginia, 16
Richwood, Ohio, 22, 104
Rockford, Ohio, 116
Rocky River, Ohio, 179
Rushville, Ohio, 131

Sabina, Ohio, 86
Sandusky, Ohio, 4, 20
Sarahsville, Ohio, 132
Scioto Valley Traction Company, 182
Shawnee, Ohio, 48, 56
Shawville, Ohio, 118
Shreve, Ohio, 46
South Charleston, Ohio, 107
Spencer, Ohio, 101, 140
Stark Electric Railway, 171, 186
Steam railroads. *See* Ohio transportation
Steubenville, Ohio, 4, 44
Stockport, Ohio, 150
Summerfield, Ohio, 133

Taft, William Howard, 158
Thurston, Ohio, 113
Tiro, Ohio, 90
Toledo, Ohio, 4, 19–20
Toledo & Indiana Railway, 188

Toledo & Ohio Central Railway, 34, 78, 83, 87–88, 95, 113, 128, 131, 148
Toledo & Western Railway, 172
Toledo, Bowling Green & Southern Traction Company, 19
Toledo, Fostoria & Findlay Railway, 23
Toledo, Port Clinton & Lakeside Railway, 192
Toledo, St. Louis & Western Railroad, 7

Uhrichsville, Ohio, 22
Unionville, Ohio, 96
Upper Sandusky, Ohio, 22
Utica, Ohio, 158

Valley Junction, Ohio, 55, 120
Van Wert, Ohio, 20

Wabash Railway, 145, 157
Waldo, Ohio, 102
Walhonding, Ohio, 74
Warren, Ohio, 137
Warren & Trumbull Railroad, 11
Warsaw Junction, Ohio, 73
Warwick, Ohio, 156
Wellington, Ohio, 142
Wellstown & Jackson Belt Railway, 185

West Alexandria, Ohio, 163
West Jefferson, Ohio, 57
Western Ohio Railway, 19, 184
Wheeling, West Virginia, 22
Wheeling & Lake Erie Railroad, 7, 10, 44, 55, 68, 89, 92, 101, 112, 120–21, 126, 134, 136. *See also* Wabash Railway
Willard, Daniel, 12
Willard, Ohio, 9, 12, 43
Willoughby, Ohio, 189, 191
Wooster, Ohio, 124

Xenia, Ohio, 103

Youngstown, Ohio, 7, 9
Youngstown & Austintown Railroad, 11
Youngstown & Ohio River, 177
Youngstown & Southern Railway, 23–24

Zanesville & Western Railroad, 13, 56, 113
Zoar, Ohio, 145

ABOUT THE AUTHOR

H. Roger Grant, Professor of History at The University of Akron, is a specialist in transportation history. He is the author, co-author, or editor of eleven books on railroads, including *Erie Lackawanna: Death of an American Railroad, 1938–1992* (Stanford University Press, 1994). Grant also edits *Railroad History,* a publication of the Railway & Locomotive Historical Society.

ABOUT THE BOOK

Ohio's Railway Age in Postcards was designed and typeset on a Macintosh in QuarkXPress by Kachergis Book Design of Pittsboro, North Carolina. The typeface is Adobe Goudy which was designed by Frederic W. Goudy (1865–1947), a former Midwestern accountant who became probably the most prolific type designer in printing history.

Ohio's Railway Age in Postcards was printed on 70-pound Sterling Litho Matte and bound in Roxite Grade A by Braun-Brumfield, Inc., Ann Arbor, Michigan.